The Life Transformation Workbook

40+ Exercises to help you Discover Your Purpose, Create Your Life Vision, and Much More!

Hunter Carson

Cover Design by Najma Imam (NinaArt)

Interior Design by Marcy McGuire

ISBN: 979-8-9854906-1-9 (ebook)

ISBN: 979-8-9854906-0-2 (Paperback)

This workbook is dedicated to the numerous coaches, teachers, and mentors I've had in my life. I would not be the person I am today without them.

Your FREE Gift

As a thanks for purchasing this workbook, I'd like to give you a copy of my book: ***17 Habits That Will Transform Your Life* for free!**

These habits are little tweaks that I have incorporated into my daily routine that have produced tremendous results in my life physically, emotionally, spiritually, mentally, and financially. By implementing most or all of these habits, you can become fitter, healthier, more focused, less stressed, become more energetic, increase your income, achieve your goals quicker, and live a better quality of life on a daily basis!

To Download this FREE PDF Book Go To:

http://huntercarsoncoaching.com/free-gift

Contents

Preface 8

How to Use This Workbook 9

Taking Action 11

Motivation for Taking Action 12

Examining How You Achieve Goals 13

Overcoming Procrastination 16

Gaining Confidence 18

Following Through 20

Identifying and Overcoming an Obstacle ...22

Solving a Recurring Problem 25

Section Takeaways 27

Wheel of Life 29

Your Wheel of Life and Closing the Gap ...30

Setting Boundaries 39

Taking Responsibility 43

Section Takeaways 44

Values + Needs 45

Finding Your Values 46

Changing Values 50

Orienting Your Life Around Your Values ...52

Discovering and Meeting Your Top Needs ...56

Developing Values and Needs 60

Section Takeaways 61

Purpose + Career 63
Discovering Your Purpose or "Why" 64
Creating Your Ideal Job Description and Dream Job 72
Section Takeaways 74

Vision + Goals 75
Creating Your Life Vision and 1 Year Goals 76
Envisioning Your Ideal Life 94
90 Day Goals in Various Areas of Life 98
Accomplish a 5 Year Goal in 6 Months 104
Setting Some SMART Goals 106
Creating a MAP (Massive Action Plan x3) 109
Make More Money 115
Section Takeaways 117

Beliefs 119
Changing Your Limiting Beliefs and Discovering Empowering Ones 120
Reviewing Important References and Gaining New Ones 125
Creating Your New Identity 127
Creating Affirmations 129
Identifying Your Life Metaphors 131
Section Takeaways 132

Emotions 133
Changing Unwanted Emotions 134
How to Feel Good Instantly 138
Energy Drains and Gains 139
Eliminating Some Stress in Your life 142
Section Takeaways 145

Habits + Routines 147
Creating a Morning Routine 148
Changing and Creating Habits 150
Changing Negative Neuro-Associations 152
Section Takeaways 154

Relationships 155
Relationship Assessment 156
Closing the Gap In a Relationship 160
Adding to Your Network 162
Relationship with Your Creator 164
Section Takeaways 166

Ending Exercises 167
Gratitude List 168
Wrapping Up What You Learned 169

Final Thoughts 174

References 175

Preface

This workbook exists because of the positive impact these exercises have had on my life and the numerous people I've shared this workbook with. Many of the other workbooks that I've come across on the market focus on purpose, or on goal-setting, or on reducing stress—but virtually none of them looked at all of these factors together. Unlike other workbooks, this workbook was designed to take all areas of your life into account, and to help you make progress on all of them simultaneously.

Changing your life, creating a life vision, discovering your values, or finding your purpose encompasses all parts and attributes of your life. It's all connected, and it all comes together in a holistic way. Focusing on one area in isolation won't get you the progress you're hoping for.

Here's an analogy to put it into perspective. Suppose you want to be healthier this year. You might start attending fitness classes, adopt a ketogenic diet, or run every day. These are all great for your physical well-being, but each one on its own won't make you healthy. To achieve that larger goal, you have to examine how all the components come together. Another way of thinking of it is that one symptom alone rarely leads to a diagnosis—a doctor needs to understand how all your symptoms, habits, and genetic predispositions are interacting first.

This workbook is designed to make you healthy in all areas of your life. Rather than focusing solely on one area, this workbook touches on every part of your life and how they work together so you can make positive changes. Through these exercises, you'll examine the various parts of your life to move toward a desired whole in a holistic way. Every area of life is interrelated with the others.

I researched hundreds or thousands of exercises to identify and develop the best of the best in their respective categories. This workbook is a culmination of that research. The exercises here encompass multiple ways of thinking about your life, and provide tangible action steps to help you make your ideal life a reality.

My goal for you is that you'll achieve at least a few major breakthroughs as you go through this workbook, and that it will support you in changing your life for the better. Each exercise has the potential to spark that breakthrough—but doing all of them will ensure you find what you need. If you take the time to think deeply and reflect on each exercise, you will gain clarity on your purpose, life vision, values, relationships, and the action steps you need to take.

How to Use This Workbook

This workbook is not necessarily meant to be read from cover to cover in the order presented, but you can certainly do that if you want.

Feel free to skip around, complete the exercises that are most enticing to you first, or complete the sections you are most intrigued by. You could think of this format as a "buffet" and you get to pick which exercises you want to do.

If you want to get a taste of each section, I would highly recommend starting with the first exercise in each section. After you finish all of those exercises, then you can go back to whatever sections or exercises you want to gain more clarity on.

This workbook is meant to be written in. Although there is space under each question to write your answers, you can write in the margins, at the top and bottom of the pages, or anywhere else you would like. Use this workbook however it works best for you.

For many people, writing can be very therapeutic. It helps us crystallize our thoughts in a tangible, visual way. It is also a vehicle for us to empty our thoughts onto paper and de-clutter our minds.

I would also recommend that you only do a few of these exercises per day. Many of them will require you to think deeply about very important aspects of your life. This isn't something that should be rushed. Take your time and make sure that you are in a creative space when going through these exercises.

Lastly, and perhaps most importantly, take action on your answers! Take action immediately. The most motivation we have for taking action is often immediately after we make a decision. Gaining awareness is great, but action is where the rubber meets the road and will help get you tangible results.

The first section, **Taking Action**, dives into how you've been both successful and unsuccessful in taking action in the past and help you pinpoint where you are hindered from making things happen.

The next section, **Wheel of Life**, touches on the various areas of your life and helps you assess where you are, where you want to be, and help you create some first steps in closing that gap.

In the third section, **Values and Needs**, you will discover what your core values and needs are and the importance they play in your decision-making. If desired, you can work to change the order of them so that they serve your goals and life vision better.

Next, you will gain much more clarity about your purpose and possible career next steps in the **Purpose and Career** section. There are several questions in this section to help you identify clues from your past and present to determine in what arenas you will be most fulfilled.

Then, you will brainstorm and work to create a life vision in the **Vision and Goals** section. Here, there are many goal setting exercises to help you create a plan for achieving various goals that align with your life vision. Remember: brainstorming is coming up with as many ideas as possible.

It doesn't matter if they seem unrealistic, farfetched, or very distant. Imagine that anything that you write will come true.

In the sixth section, **Beliefs**, you get to define what some empowering and limiting beliefs are for you in your life. You will work to eradicate the limiting ones and work to create a new paradigm for how you see yourself and the world around you.

Next is **Emotions.** Here you get to discover what your most common emotions are and create plans and strategies to limit the amount of time you experience negative ones, and increase the amount of time you experience positive ones.

The next section is **Habits and Routines**. Here you will create a morning routine and work to replace negative habits and create some positive ones.

Then there is the **Relationships** section. There are a few exercises here to help you assess where you are in various relationships (including your relationship to God), and help you create a plan for where you'd like to be in these areas.

Finally, you'll get to wrap up and reflect on what all you've learned in the last section.

Again, feel free to skip around to different sections, or start with the ones that you feel you need help in the most. Use this workbook how you'd like so that it serves you best!

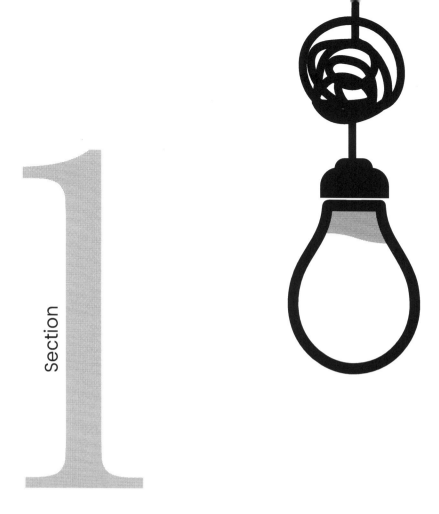

Taking Action

P lanning is great. Self-awareness is helpful. Ideas have lots of potential. However, none of it matters if you don't take action. Action is where the rubber meets the road, where thoughts get converted into physical form, where things actually happen.

Regardless of what insights or breakthroughs you create while working through this workbook, you won't be successful without taking action on them. That's why this section is first.

Here, you'll reflect on how you've successfully taken action in the past, how you can navigate procrastination and overcome obstacles more easily, and generate motivation for taking action.

Motivation for Taking Action

What are at least 5 things that have motivated you to take action in the past? Examples could be music, watching a video, exercising, or reading a book.

_____

_____

_____

_____

_____

_____

What are 5 things that consistently hinder you from taking action?

_____

_____

_____

_____

_____

How can you add more of the things that motivate you to take action into your life? How can you reduce the things that hinder your motivation for taking action? How can you implement these into your daily or weekly routines?

_____

_____

_____

_____

_____

_____

_____

Examining How You Achieve Goals

Think about some prior goals you achieved to see if you can find any parallels or tips that will help you hit your current objectives.

What are some prior goals that you have achieved that you felt very proud about?

_____

_____

_____

_____

What led to achieving your goals? What did you have in place to support your success?

_____

_____

_____

_____

_____

_____

If you ever felt like giving up or not taking action on these goals, what kept you persevering?

_____

_____

_____

_____

_____

How did you overcome procrastination with these goals?

_____

_____

_____

_____

_____

When was it hard to get motivated to take action? Why? When was it easy to get motivated to take action? Why?

_____

_____

_____

_____

_____

How did others help you with this goal?

_____

_____

_____

_____

How did it feel when you achieved these goals?

_____

_____

_____

_____

What have you learned from hitting your past goals that you can apply to achieve your current ones?

Overcoming Procrastination

We all suffer from procrastination to some degree. To overcome the tendency to procrastinate, we must first become aware of the problem, condition ourselves to associate completing tasks with pleasure and procrastination with pain, and then practice.

What are at least 3 decisions that you've either put off, or haven't had the courage to make, that will positively change your life?

_____

_____

_____

_____

_____

What pain have you associated with taking these actions in the past or up until now?

_____

_____

_____

_____

What have you gained from NOT taking these actions or following through with them?

_____

_____

_____

_____

_____

What will it cost you if you don't follow through now or soon?

_____

_____

_____

_____

_____

What will you gain, or what pleasure will you get from taking these actions now?

_____

_____

_____

_____

What are some reasons that you MUST change now, and why you know you can?

_____

_____

_____

_____

_____

_____

Lastly, put the actions you'll take on your calendar. Include how and when you will take these actions if you are committed to them.

Gaining Confidence

Having confidence is essential to achieving your goals and living up to the best version of yourself. Regardless of your vocation, who doesn't want to be confident in what they do and who they are? This exercise will help you envision what a high level of confidence will look like for you.

If you had all the confidence in the world, what would you do? How would you carry yourself?

_____

_____

_____

_____

_____

_____

What has impacted your confidence most? What builds it up and what tears it down?

_____

_____

_____

_____

What opportunities would you pursue if you had more confidence?

_____

_____

_____

_____

How could you develop more confidence in your life? What practical things could you do?

Following Through

What are the most common reasons you fail to follow through or complete a task or goal? What stories or excuses do you tell yourself? List at least 5 reasons.

_____

_____

_____

_____

_____

How can you replace these excuses to take action? What are some of the things you can do, tell yourself, or believe?

_____

_____

_____

_____

_____

List some things that you are struggling to follow through with currently, or some recent failures you want to correct.

_____

_____

_____

_____

_____

Next, come up with a list of actions you can take that will help you produce results.

_____

_____

_____

_____

_____

_____

_____

Why must you take these actions? How committed are you to doing them? How will you feel after the actions are completed?

_____

_____

_____

_____

_____

What reward can you give yourself after taking these actions?

_____

_____

_____

_____

_____

Identifying and Overcoming an Obstacle

We usually know what we need to do to hit a goal, but actually doing it can be much harder than what it seems. Often, obstacles come up, and to succeed we need to navigate them.

What is a goal or problem you are struggling to conquer?

_____

_____

_____

What is stopping you from conquering it? What makes the obstacle challenging?

_____

_____

_____

_____

What do you need that you don't have to reach your objective? How could you access that resource?

_____

_____

_____

What external factors will you need to account for if you are going to conquer this goal or problem? What one resource or tool would make all the difference if you had it?

_____

_____

_____

_____

What do you gain by NOT conquering this problem or goal? What do you lose?

_____

_____

_____

_____

_____

_____

When you've faced obstacles like this in the past, how did you overcome them?

_____

_____

_____

_____

_____

What are at least 5 solutions you could implement to overcome this obstacle?

_____

_____

_____

_____

_____

_____

Which of these solutions will you implement first? Why?

_____

_____

_____

What resources do you need to conquer this obstacle? Where could you get them?

_____

_____

_____

Solving a Recurring Problem

What is the most important recurring problem that you want to solve right now?

_____

_____

What would make a lasting difference and not just a temporary one? What would it look like to conquer this once and for all?

_____

_____

_____

_____

Is this a one time issue for you or something you struggle with a lot? What obstacles to change have you run into in this area?

_____

_____

_____

_____

What in this situation or problem is within your control that you can realistically change? How could you change your response to this problem?

_____

_____

_____

_____

_____

How can you eliminate this problem once and for all? What would need to be done? What resources could you tap into to help you here?

_____

_____

_____

_____

_____

_____

Think of other problems that you could solve once and for all. Create a plan below.

_____

_____

_____

_____

_____

_____

_____

_____

_____

_____

_____

_____

Section Takeaways

What insights, breakthroughs, takeaways, and actionable items did you get from the above section?

NOTES

_____

_____

_____

_____

_____

_____

_____

_____

_____

_____

_____

_____

_____

_____

_____

_____

_____

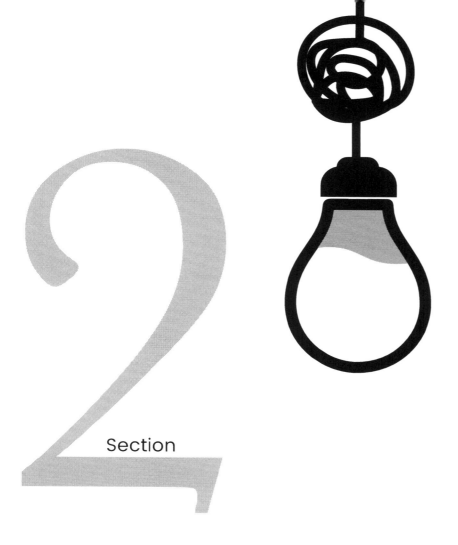

Section

2

Wheel of Life

T he Wheel of Life is a common tool used by life coaches that can help you assess the current status of various life categories. A well-rounded wheel indicates that your life is balanced in all areas, while an uneven wheel signifies that life isn't rolling along as smoothly—or that you're having a rocky ride.

Too few people take the time to assess how each aspect of their life is going. Often, we focus on a couple of areas, like finances or relationships, but seldom do we evaluate all areas together. This means that most people lack a holistic sense of how their life is going: they may sense that the ride isn't smooth, but they can't figure out what's not working.

In this section, you will analyze your own Wheel of Life, think about where you want to be by the end of the next 12-18 months, and develop a plan for closing those gaps. Specifically, you'll think about taking action, setting boundaries, and taking ownership over each area of your life.

Your Wheel of Life and Closing the Gap[1]

On a scale of 1-10, rate your current level of satisfaction with each of the following areas of life (1=completely unsatisfied, 10=completely satisfied).

Underneath each rating, write 2-4 bullet points giving the reason for the number you chose.

Health + Body _____

Career/Business _____

Finances _____

Relationships/Family _____

Time Management _____

Emotions _____

Social/Fun/Self-Care _____

Personal/Spiritual Development _____

---

1   Robbins, T. (2020). *The gap map*. Retrieved April 14, 2021, from https://gapmap.tonyrobbins.com/

How many hours in an average week do you think you spend focusing on each area? Assume you have approximately 100 hours to distribute among the areas. There are 168 hours per week, so the remaining hours can be allotted for sleeping, eating, errands, etc.

Health + Body _____

Career/Business _____

Finances _____

Relationships/Family _____

Time Management _____

Emotions _____

Social/Fun/Self-Care _____

Personal/Spiritual Development _____

Which area is most important to you right now? Why?

_____

_____

_____

_____

_____

_____

Which area(s) causes you the most stress? Why do you think that is?

_____

_____

_____

_____

_____

_____

In what area(s) are you spending too much time, and in what area(s) are you spending too little? Which area(s) is sapping too much of your time and energy?

_____

_____

_____

On a scale of 1-10, rate what you want your level of satisfaction to be in each area in the next 12 months (1=completely unsatisfied, 10=completely satisfied).

Underneath each rating, write 2-4 bullet points explaining what it would look like and what you would need to do to reach that satisfaction level.

Physical Health + Body _____

Career/Business _____

Finances _____

Relationships/Family _____

Time Management _____

Emotions _____

Social/Fun/Self-Care _____

Personal/Spiritual Development _____

How many hours on an average week would you like to spend in each category? Again, allocate approximately 100 hours.

Health + Body _____

Career/Business _____

Finances _____

Relationships/Family_____

Time Management _____

Emotions _____

Social/Fun/Self-Care_____

Personal/Spiritual Development _____

Which area do you want to be most important to you? Why?

_____

_____

_____

_____

_____

_____

When you compare the two lists (where you are versus where you want to be), what stands out? How does your current life align with where you want to be? Which area(s) are you pleased with?

_____

_____

_____

_____

_____

_____

_____

_____

Where are the gaps in where you are versus where you want to be? What are the biggest actions you could take to close these gaps?

_____

_____

_____

_____

_____

_____

_____

Do you feel balanced?

If not, what areas need attention? What can you do about it? What activities or commitments do you need to cut out of your life? What activities could you do to make your life more balanced?

_____

_____

_____

_____

_____

_____

_____

Out of all these areas, which 1-2 do you want to focus on MOST the next 12 or so months?

_____   _____

Let's get more clarity and direction on these areas. Let's start with the first area you want to improve most over the next 12 months.

In the space below, expand on the current status of this area of your life. Try to be as honest and specific as possible.

_____

_____

_____

_____

_____

What outcomes or results would you like in this area of your life? Try to be specific and include items that are measurable and quantifiable.

_____

_____

_____

Why do you want these results? How will you feel once you achieve this? How committed are you to creating this outcome?

_____

_____

_____

_____

What resources could you utilize to help you attain this outcome? (Some examples could be people, books, coaching, etc.)

_____

_____

_____

Who or what can help hold you accountable to achieving these results? What environments would support you?

_____

_____

_____

What actions do you need to take on a consistent basis to close the gap here? What actions in general do you need to take to achieve this goal? Are there any habits that you need to establish?

_____

_____

_____

_____

Circle the top 3-5 actions you need to take to close the gap. Then schedule them! Put them on your calendar **RIGHT NOW**!

What beliefs do you currently have about this area of your life that are either limiting, false, or disempowering?

_____

_____

_____

What are some beliefs you have or could adopt that will empower you in this area going forward?

_____

_____

_____

What is your vision, your most compelling reason, to close the gap in this area? What will your identity be when you achieve what you want in this area?

_____

_____

_____

_____

Now, if applicable, let's expand on the second area of your life you'd like to improve most over the next 12 months.

In the space below, expand on the current status of this area of your life. Try to be as honest and specific as possible.

_____

_____

_____

_____

What outcomes or results would you like in this area of your life? Try to be specific and include items that are measurable and quantifiable.

_____

_____

_____

Why do you want these results? How will you feel once you achieve this? How committed are you to creating this outcome?

_____

_____

_____

What resources could you utilize to help you attain this outcome? (Some examples could be people, books, coaching, etc.)

_____

_____

_____

Who or what can help hold you accountable to achieving these results? What environments would support you?

_____

_____

_____

What actions do you need to take on a consistent basis to close the gap here? What actions in general do you need to take to achieve this goal? Are there any habits that you need to establish?

_____

_____

_____

_____

Circle the top 3-5 actions you need to take to close the gap. Then schedule them! Put them on your calendar **RIGHT NOW!**

What beliefs do you currently have about this area of your life that are either limiting, false, or disempowering?

_____

_____

_____

What are some beliefs you have or could adopt that will empower you in this area going forward?

_____

_____

_____

What is your vision, your most compelling reason, to close the gap in this area? What will your identity be when you achieve what you want in this area?

_____

_____

_____

_____

Setting Boundaries

Boundaries can serve as pre-meditated decisions in various scenarios to help you stay on track with your goals. They help you automate decisions ahead of time so you don't have to think on the spot when your willpower might be weaker. Think about all the areas of your life from the Wheel of Life exercise. In what areas do you need to set better boundaries? What boundaries do you need to create in the following areas?

In addition to setting boundaries, think of situations, circumstances, or people you need to say no to more often. How can you plan your responses in these areas?

For example, suppose I want to lose weight. However, I'm going out to eat 3 nights a week with work colleagues, when I almost always make unhealthy food and drink choices. A boundary I could set here is to limit the number of times I go out with my work colleagues per week, and I could practice saying no to unhealthy meals and drinks when I do.

List your own ideas below:

Health + Body

_____

_____

_____

_____

_____

Career/Business

_____

_____

_____

_____

_____

Finances

_____

_____

_____

_____

_____

_____

Relationships

_____

_____

_____

_____

_____

_____

Time Management

_____

_____

_____

_____

_____

_____

Emotions

_____

_____

_____

_____

_____

Social/Fun/Self-Care

_____

_____

_____

_____

_____

Personal/Spiritual Development

_____

_____

_____

_____

_____

Out of all these areas, which one do you most need boundaries in or need to say no in most? Why?

_____

_____

_____

What will it cost you to NOT set boundaries and say no more often? What do you gain by setting boundaries?

_____

_____

_____

_____

_____

What boundaries are most important for you to establish right now?

_____

_____

_____

_____

Who or what currently violates these boundaries?

_____

_____

_____

_____

What actions can you take to enforce these boundaries? How can you be proactive in implementing them?

_____

_____

_____

_____

Taking Responsibility

No matter what happens in life, you can take responsibility for how you react. It's vital to take ownership of whatever problems you encounter, and any situations you find yourself in. Adopting this mindset will reinforce that fact that we ALWAYS have the power to change a situation or solve a problem. Rather than spending time blaming others, focus on what you can do to create change and get the results you want.

Think back to the Wheel of Life categories. In what area of your life do you need to take more responsibility? Why?

_____

_____

_____

What specifically do you need to take more responsibility or ownership of?

_____

_____

_____

What actions could you take to be more responsible here? What structures or systems could you put in place?

_____

_____

_____

How would taking these actions and taking more responsibility here affect your life?

_____

_____

_____

43

Section Takeaways

What insights, breakthroughs, takeaways, and actionable items did you get from the above section?

Section

3

Values + Needs

Understanding your values and needs will help you develop greater self-awareness. Values and needs shape almost every decision that you make, and thus have a major effect on your life. They are like an internal compass guiding you through your voyage of life.

Gaining awareness of your values and needs will help you make decisions much easier. Often, indecision is the result of conflicts related to your values or needs.

In this section, you will identify your primary values and needs. Then, if desired, you can work to change them so that they serve you better in creating the life you want, or the person you want to become.

Finding Your Values[2]

First, we're going to focus on what are called your **moving-toward values**. These are positive values, values that you aspire to have, and values associated with peace, pleasure, and happiness. It's helpful to look at these values first when making important decisions.

Here are some questions that may help you think of your moving-toward values:

- What are the emotional states that you appreciate most in life?

- What emotions give you the most pleasure?

- What feelings are important for you to experience consistently?

Here is a list of several common values, but please note that there are others beyond this list:

Love	Significance	Humor	Tidiness
Success	Variety	Influence	Thrill
Freedom	Respect	Optimism	Impact
Intimacy	Intelligence	Wealth	Coaching
Security	Honesty	Integrity	Teaching
Adventure	Gratefulness	Family	Serving
Power	Competitiveness	Responsibility	Creating
Passion	Loyalty	Harmony	Planning
Comfort	Courage	Spontaneity	Leading
Health	Authenticity	Inspiration	Superiority
Peace	Balance	Community	Integrity
Contribution	Beauty	Compassion	Connection
Growth	Challenge	Serving	Spirituality
Faith	Community	Generosity	Winning
Achievement	Curiosity	Recognition	Acceptance
Happiness	Justice	Efficiency	Discipline
Fun	Determination	Excellence	Practicality
Creativity	Friendship	Reputation	Resourcefulness

2   Robbins, A. (2013). *Awaken the giant within: How to take immediate control of your mental, emotional, physical & financial destiny!* New York: Simon & Schuster Paperbacks.

In the space below, brainstorm as many moving-toward values as you can. These are states, emotions, and qualities that you are naturally drawn to in life.

From the list, circle the 10 or so values that are **MOST IMPORTANT** to you.

Now, you will rank those 10 values in order of importance, with 1 being the most important value to you.

When deciding the order of values, it can be helpful to compare them side by side. For example, suppose I have Success and Balance as important values in my life. I must ask myself which one I would rather have. Which of these values has higher importance in my life if I had to choose between the two?

If you are having trouble ranking your values, consider asking a few people who know you really well to rank these for you. This can also give you some insight about your value's priority and how you're actually living that value out.

Rank your values below:

What do each of these values mean to you?

_____

_____

_____

_____

Next, we are going to find your **moving-away from values.** You avoid these values because they tend to bring pain to your life.

Here are some questions that may help you think of your moving-away from values:

- What emotions or states do you typically avoid on a consistent basis?

- What emotions or states bring you pain?

Here is a list of some common moving-away values. Again, there are far more values than from this list below.

Rejection	Humiliation	Discomfort	Inadequacy
Anger	Guilt	Stress	Disappointment
Frustration	Negativity	Fear	Regret
Loneliness	Procrastination	Anxiety	Rejection
Depression	Pain	Insecurity	
Failure	Evil	Embarrassment	

Brainstorm a list of moving-away from values in the space below.

_____

_____

_____

_____

_____

_____

_____

From the list circle the 5 or so moving-away from values that you *AVOID* most. These values typically bring you lots of pain.

Now, you will rank the moving-away from values in the order of which ones you want to avoid most, with 1 being the one you avoid most.

Again, when deciding the order of values, it is helpful to compare them side by side. For example, suppose I have Rejection and Guilt as a couple moving-away from values. I must ask myself which one I would rather avoid most. Which of these two values would I avoid more when comparing them next to each other?

If you are having trouble ranking these, consider asking a few people who know you really well to rank these for you.

Rank your moving-away from values hierarchy below:

What do each of these values mean to you?

What have you discovered about yourself from this exercise? How do you feel about your values hierarchies?

Changing Values

Although it is important to know what your values currently are, sometimes they may not serve your goals or support the person you want to become. This exercise will help you change the values that are no longer serving you. First, please complete the Find Your Values exercise if you haven't already done so.

Here is a list of several common values, but please note that there are others beyond this list:

Love	Significance	Humor	Tidiness
Success	Variety	Influence	Thrill
Freedom	Respect	Optimism	Impact
Intimacy	Intelligence	Wealth	Coaching
Security	Honesty	Integrity	Teaching
Adventure	Gratefulness	Family	Serving
Power	Competitiveness	Responsibility	Creating
Passion	Loyalty	Harmony	Planning
Comfort	Courage	Spontaneity	Leading
Health	Authenticity	Inspiration	Superiority
Peace	Balance	Community	Integrity
Contribution	Beauty	Compassion	Connection
Growth	Challenge	Serving	Spirituality
Faith	Community	Generosity	Winning
Achievement	Curiosity	Recognition	Acceptance
Happiness	Justice	Efficiency	Discipline
Fun	Determination	Excellence	Practicality
Creativity	Friendship	Reputation	Resourcefulness

Brainstorm a list of values that you need to have to achieve your goals, life vision, purpose, and be the best version of yourself.

Are there any values that you should add or eliminate from your list above?

Using these values, circle the top *10 or so most important values* you need to have to hit your goals and become the person you desire.

Now, you will decide the hierarchy of the values you need to have to hit your goals and be the best version of yourself.

Consider asking these questions when deciding your values hierarchy:

• What order do my values need to be in, if I am to achieve my life vision and goals?

• What benefit do I get by having each value in this position?

• What could having this value here cost me?

Rank your values in order of importance, with 1 being the most important.

_____

_____

_____

_____

_____

_____

_____

Take a picture of this list and keep it in a place that you will see every day. It's very important that you review your values DAILY until you can easily rehearse them. When you know your values hierarchy, it's much easier to make decisions.

Orienting Your Life Around Your Values

Look back at your calendar from the past few months. Make a list of all the activities you participate in during an average week.

_____

_____

_____

_____

_____

_____

_____

_____

_____

_____

_____

_____

_____

_____

Next, using your current or desired new values, write the value next to each activity where that value is utilized. For example, if I exercise in the mornings, I could put Health or Vitality next to that activity.

What activities are you doing where you are living out your core values?

_____

_____

_____

_____

_____

_____

What activities don't align with any of your values?

_____

_____

_____

_____

_____

_____

How do your actions and activities on an average week align with your values? Which values are underutilized?

_____

_____

_____

_____

_____

_____

How can you eliminate, delegate, or automate some of the activities that don't serve your top values? What on your calendar blocks your core values and how can you reduce or eliminate those blocks?

_____

_____

_____

_____

_____

_____

_____

_____

What activities could you add into your schedule so you become more aligned with your core values? Are there any activities you could modify?

_____

_____

_____

_____

_____

_____

_____

_____

Brainstorm a list of several habits that would help you express your values more fully on a consistent basis.

_____

_____

_____

_____

_____

_____

_____

Circle 2-3 habits from the list to start implementing in your life right now!

How would you feel if you were to live out your top core values on a more consistent basis? What if your life was exclusively oriented around your core values?

_____

_____

_____

_____

What will it cost you to not add or eliminate some of these activities and habits?

_____

_____

_____

_____

Why are you committed to making these changes in your life?

_____

_____

_____

_____

Discovering and Meeting Your Top Needs[3]

As humans, we all have needs that must be met. When our needs go unmet, we feel unsatisfied, out of alignment, or unhappy with our overall life conditions. The most basic and essential needs are air, water, food, and warmth. Beyond those, we also crave a safe, secure environment. However, after the basic needs are met, there are still other needs that must be satisfied for us to reach happiness and fulfillment.

Some of the most common needs are: *Certainty/Security, Variety, Significance, Satisfaction, Connection or Love, Growth, and Contribution.*

We all prioritize these 7 needs in different ways. In this section, we will determine how these needs are currently being met in your life, their order of importance for you, and how to get them met more consistently.

We all have a degree of **certainty/security** we must have in our lives to feel safe. When this need is unmet, we feel very fearful. Life can be very painful and full of suffering if we are fearful all the time. How do you try to get **certainty** in your life?

_____

_____

_____

_____

_____

_____

If everything in our lives remained certain all the time, we would probably get bored. For that reason, we all need some degree of **variety** in our life. How do you try to get **variety** in your life?

_____

_____

_____

_____

_____

3   Robbins, A. (2017). *Ultimate edge a three part system for creating an extraordinary life in any environment*. San Diego, CA: Robbins Research International.

We all have a need to feel that we are unique in some way—that our lives have a special purpose, meaning, or **significance**. How do you try to get **significance** in your life? List some of the things you do that make you feel unique, needed, fulfilled, or significant.

_____

_____

_____

_____

_____

Everybody wants to experience **satisfaction**—to gain pleasure or avoid pain. Being satisfied means that some or many of your desires have been met. How do you try to get **satisfaction** in your life?

_____

_____

_____

_____

_____

Next, we all want to feel **connection or love** with others and with the world around us. How do you try to get **connection and love** in your life? List some of the ways you try to feel connected to yourself, to others, the world, or to your Creator.

_____

_____

_____

_____

_____

Life wouldn't be very fun if there wasn't much opportunity for **growth**. If we didn't learn anything, were never tested, or failed, life would be boring, whether that's related to work, personal development, relationships, etc. How do you try to get **growth** in your life?

_____

_____

_____

_____

_____

Lastly, we all have a deep need to go beyond ourselves to live a life that **contributes** to others and the greater good. How do you try to **contribute** in your life?

_____

_____

_____

_____

_____

Next, let's prioritize your needs. Please rank them in the importance that each plays in your life from 1-7.
Again, it may be helpful to compare each need side by side with another one. If you had to choose between growth and significance, which need is more important to be met for you?

Certainty _____

Variety _____

Significance _____

Connection/Love _____

Satisfaction _____

Growth _____

Contribution _____

Now that you have prioritized your needs, do you see any conflicts in the order?

For example, if your top 2 needs are certainty and growth, you might see that there is a conflict. It's hard to grow if certainty is such a big factor, because growing often requires getting out of your comfort zone.

_____

_____

_____

_____

What are 5 specific ways your life is better with having these needs met?

_____

_____

_____

_____

_____

Which need(s) is currently unsatisfied? Why?

_____

_____

What actions or systems can you put in place so your needs will be satisfied on a regular basis?

_____

_____

_____

_____

What if you permanently satisfied these needs? How would that affect your life? What would need to happen for these needs to be permanently or regularly met?

_____

_____

Developing Values and Needs

What values, needs, or traits do you want to develop in yourself most right now? Why?

_____

_____

_____

_____

_____

How could you do this? What are some action steps you could take?

_____

_____

_____

_____

_____

_____

Who can hold you accountable to this? How can they hold you accountable?

_____

_____

Why are you committed to developing these qualities? What will it cost you if you don't, and what will you gain if you do develop them?

_____

_____

_____

_____

Section Takeaways

What insights, breakthroughs, takeaways, and actionable items did you get from the above section?

NOTES

Purpose + Career

T hose of us who live in the U.S. spend so much of our lives devoted to our jobs. Almost half of our waking hours are spent on work—and 87% of American employees aren't engaged at their jobs, according to one Gallup poll. That's a big problem.

If you're going to devote so much of your time to work, why wouldn't you want to do things that are aligned with who you are at your core, and that bring you joy and fulfillment? As Stephen Covey wrote in The 7 Habits of Highly Effective People, "Better to be at the bottom of a ladder you want to climb than at the top of some ladder you don't, right?"

In this section, you will gain a much better awareness of what your purpose is, and what your next career step might be. Although this section only has a couple of exercises, they are powerful. Take your time working through these longer exercises, and you'll find the benefits unmistakable.

Discovering Your Purpose or "Why"

To discover our purpose—our "why," or our reason for doing things—we need to look at our pasts, character traits, and personalities. Answering the following questions will give you some clues as to what your purpose is.

The following questions will help you connect the dots from your past to your present, and reveal the patterns, skills, and influences that contribute to finding your purpose.

List 5-10 examples of times when you felt like you were living on purpose. Perhaps it was a specific day or experience where you felt like you were doing what you were born to do. It might be an experience where you felt fully alive, you were firing on all cylinders, or you were in a flow state. Write a little about each example: what about the experience was satisfying, what value did it have for you, and what aligned it with your purpose?

_____

_____

_____

_____

_____

_____

_____

_____

What stands out to you from the experiences you listed? What do they have in common? Which details were crucial to your impact or fulfillment? What made them significant to you?

_____

_____

_____

_____

_____

Where have you found real purpose in your life?

How did your childhood (or activities you did in your childhood) influence your purpose? Were there any specific activities that you enjoyed that might relate to your purpose?

What experiences have most shaped who you are as a person? What turning points have you experienced in your life that may have pushed you toward your life purpose?

What have your failures and missteps qualified you to do? What gifts have your failures given you?

What do you know about your personality? What have you learned from personality assessments?

_____

_____

_____

What type of environments do you thrive in? What kind of people do you enjoy being around?

_____

_____

_____

_____

_____

_____

What relationships or people have influenced your sense of purpose? How so?

_____

_____

_____

_____

_____

_____

What influence has your family had on your purpose? What clues (if any) are present in your family that might reveal what your purpose is?

_____

_____

_____

_____

_____

_____

Is there anyone in your family who you think you may have a similar purpose to? What can you learn about your family origins about yourself?

_____

_____

_____

What have you been passionate about in your life so far, or, what are some things you are very curious about?

_____

_____

_____

Circle the one that has been the most meaningful and inspirational for you.

What motivates you? What are some things that give you lots of energy?

_____

_____

_____

_____

_____

What brings you the most joy, pleasure, and satisfaction in life? What do you love to do or what have you loved to do?

_____

_____

_____

What are you great at? What are your best talents and abilities? Is there anything that comes easy for you?

_____

_____

_____

What are some things that you can do in a unique way that no one else can do?

_____

_____

_____

_____

What talents or skills make you feel most alive and joyful when you use them?

_____

_____

_____

_____

What knowledge or skills have you acquired in your career that you want to incorporate as you pursue your purpose in life?

_____

_____

_____

_____

What roles or jobs have excited you in the past? Which ones have you hated? Why do you think that is?

_____

_____

_____

_____

List 3 specific aspects that would be part of your ideal job. What makes these aspects important?

_____

_____

_____

If 5 of your closest friends had to pick an ideal job for you, what might they say?

What do you feel has been revealed to you about your own destiny or calling? Do you have any spiritual experiences that are related to your purpose?

Who do you want to help in your life? What kinds of people would you most like to make a difference for?

What do you care most about that is bigger than you? This could be a cause, principle, goal, truth, etc. What are some things that you stand for?

If you could spend your life working to change one thing in the world that would make a real difference to others, what would it be? If you can't limit it to one, what are a few?

_____

_____

_____

_____

Why do you think you are drawn to this?

_____

_____

_____

What are some of your dreams? If you could have, do, or be anything you want, what would it be?

_____

_____

_____

_____

What do you already know about what your purpose is in life, what you were made to do, or what you are not made to do?

_____

_____

_____

_____

What do you feel life has prepared you to do? What does it seem like your life has been leading up to?

_____

_____

_____

_____

_____

Now, go back and look through all your answers from the above questions. Look for themes, patterns, repetitive words or phrases, key words, etc.

From all the above questions, which 3-5 main points stand out? How do these reflect on what you think your purpose is?

_____

_____

_____

_____

_____

Finally, work to draft a couple sentences that explain your purpose, drawing from the themes, words, and phrases from the above questions. Think of this as your personal "why" or mission statement.

A helpful format to use is:

To _____ so that _____.

For example, Simon Sinek (author of Start with Why) says his "why" is, "To inspire people to do the things that inspire them so, together, each of us can change our world for the better."

_____

_____

_____

Review this statement often and keep editing it until you find something that sticks. It will resonate with you on a gut level once you have it.

Creating Your Ideal Job Description and Dream Job

In this exercise, you will brainstorm an ideal job description. Remember that brainstorming doesn't necessarily have to be realistic, just write whatever comes to mind for you. You can connect this exercise with your insights from the previous exercise if you'd like.

In the space below, write your ideal job description.

What are the responsibilities? What qualities and experiences are required? What would the ideal candidate have? What would they be passionate about?

_____

_____

_____

_____

_____

_____

Brainstorm a list of all the jobs, careers, or professions you would like to do if you had no restrictions (financial, location, education, etc.). If you knew you couldn't fail, what would you do?

_____

_____

_____

What are some realistic job options that align with what you wrote?

_____

_____

_____

_____

_____

_____

Next, rank each job, career, or profession from the list above in each of the following categories: ease, cost, effect on your family, effect on your life, and your excitement about that job.

For this exercise, use a scale of 1-5 where 1 represents the greatest level of ease and excitement, and the lowest level of cost and effects; 5 should represent the lowest level of ease and excitement, and the highest level of cost and effects.

Job	Ease	Cost	Family Effect	Personal/Life Effect	Excitement	Total

What can you deduce from the chart above? Is there one job in particular that makes the most sense to you? Which one has the lowest score (meaning that it would be the easiest to do or would have the lowest effect on your life)?

If applicable, what action steps could you take to pivot into one of the jobs you have picked from above?

Section Takeaways

What insights, breakthroughs, takeaways, and actionable items did you get from the above section?

5

Vision + Goals

Just like a builder can't build a house or structure without a blueprint, it will be impossible for you to build your life without a map or model to draw from. Unfortunately, most people don't think too much about what they want their life to look like, and therefore aren't living their ideal life. They never take the time to draw the blueprint for their lives.

Luckily for us, we are powerful creatures. What we create in our mind, we can turn into reality. We can create a map for our ideal lives and follow it until we get the result we wanted.

Simply writing down what your ideal life may look like greatly enhances your chances of making it happen. Writing down your goals and vision means you establish a target that you can now work toward—so the more specific you can be, the better.

In this section, you will map out and create a blueprint for all areas of your life. You will get specific on what you want your life to look like and then set goals to take action.

Creating Your Life Vision and 1 Year Goals[4]

In this exercise, you will describe your life vision for several different categories. This is a powerful exercise, and one that has the potential to change the course of your life.

I highly recommend setting aside a full hour to do this exercise. Work on these questions in a place where you won't be disturbed, and where you can let your creative juices flow.

Remember: brainstorming is coming up with as many ideas as possible. It doesn't matter if they seem unrealistic, farfetched, or very distant. Imagine that anything that you write will come true.

---

4   Robbins, A. (2013). *Awaken the giant within: How to take immediate control of your mental, emotional, physical & financial destiny!* New York: Simon & Schuster Paperbacks.

Personal Growth

In the space below, brainstorm everything in your life you would like to improve regarding your **personal growth**. This could include skills, traits, spiritual goals, physical goals, health aspirations, things to learn, etc.

This exercise can be challenging. If that's the case, consider asking yourself these questions to get you started: What have I done in the past in this area of my life that has been truly satisfying? What would happen if I did more of that?

Next, circle the one, that if it came true, would have the biggest impact on your life in the next 12 or so months.

In the space below, write how achieving this goal will impact your life. What would it mean to you to reach this goal? What difference would it make? What emotions would you experience if you reached this goal?

_____

_____

_____

_____

_____

_____

Next, brainstorm all the actions that you need to take to achieve this goal. Create a strategy for achieving this.

_____

_____

_____

_____

_____

_____

_____

_____

_____

_____

Circle the 3 most important actions that would move you closer to achieving your goal.

Finally, if necessary, write all the additional actions you will need to take to complete each of the items you circled in the previous question. This will be your action plan.

For example, if my top goal was to lose 50 pounds this year, one of my actions might be to eat 1500 calories per day. To put that action into practice, I may need to track everything I eat, create a weekly diet, and meal prep.

Now put these actions on your calendar **RIGHT NOW.** Don't delay. You've already made a commitment; take action on it immediately!

Career, Business, or Financial Life

In the space below, brainstorm everything in your life you want for your **career, business, or financial life.** This could include how much you want to earn per year, how much to save/invest to retire, when you want to retire, company goals, career goals, what type of investments you would like to make, money management goals, etc.

This exercise can be challenging. If that's the case, consider asking yourself these questions to get you started: What have I done in the past in this area of my life that has been truly satisfying? What would happen if I did more of that?

_____

_____

_____

_____

_____

_____

_____

_____

_____

_____

_____

_____

_____

_____

Next, circle the one, that if it came true, would have the biggest impact on your life in the next 12 or so months.

In the space below, write how achieving this goal will impact your life. What would it mean to you to reach this goal? What difference would it make? What emotions would you experience if you reached this goal?

_____

_____

_____

_____

_____

Next, brainstorm all the actions that you need to take to achieve this goal. Create a strategy for achieving this.

_____

_____

_____

_____

_____

_____

_____

_____

_____

_____

_____

Circle the 3 most important actions that would move you closer to achieving your goal.

Finally, if necessary, write all the additional actions you will need to take to complete each of the items you circled in the previous question. This will be your action plan.

For example, if my top goal was to start a new consulting business, one of my top actions would be to get a loan for the venture. Here I could write: Talk to 20 banks in my area, make a list of all family and friends to reach out to about investing with me, and research other sources of funding.

_____

_____

_____

_____

_____

_____

_____

_____

_____

_____

_____

_____

_____

_____

_____

Now put these actions on your calendar **RIGHT NOW.** Don't delay. You've already made a commitment; take action on it immediately!

Relationships

In the space below, brainstorm everything in your life you would like to have regarding your relationships. This could include **relationships** with your spouse or significant other, friends, family, work colleagues, or your relationship with your Creator.

This exercise can be challenging. If that's the case, consider asking yourself these questions to get you started: What have I done in the past in this area of my life that has been truly satisfying? What would happen if I did more of that?

Next, circle the one, that if it came true, would have the biggest impact on your life in the next 12 months.

In the space below, write how achieving this goal will impact your life. What would it mean to you to reach this goal? What difference would it make? What emotions would you experience if you reached this goal?

_____

_____

_____

_____

Next brainstorm all the actions that you need to take to achieve this goal. Create a strategy for achieving this.

_____

_____

_____

_____

_____

_____

_____

_____

_____

_____

_____

_____

Circle the 3 most important actions that would move you closer to achieving your goal.

Finally, if necessary, write all the additional actions you will need to take to complete each of the items you circled in the above space. This will be your action plan.

For example, if my top goal was to have a 10/10 marriage, one of my top actions might be to spend more time with my spouse weekly. Here I could include scheduling at least one date per week and spending a minimum of one hour together after work every day doing something we both enjoy.

_____

_____

_____

_____

_____

_____

_____

_____

_____

_____

_____

_____

Now put these actions on your calendar **RIGHT NOW**. Don't delay. You've already made a commitment; take action on it immediately!

Adventure/Toys/Fun

In the space below, brainstorm everything in your life you want regarding **adventure, toys, and fun.** This could include some of the things you'd like to have, some of the places you'd like to see, activities you'd like to do, or experiences you'd like to have.

This exercise can be challenging. If that's the case, consider asking yourself these questions to get you started: What have I done in the past in this area of my life that has been truly satisfying? What would happen if I did more of that?

Next, circle the one, that if it came true, would have the biggest impact on your life in the next 12 months.

In the space below, write how achieving this goal will impact your life. What would it mean to you to reach this goal? What difference would it make? What emotions would you experience if you reached this goal?

Next brainstorm all the actions that you need to take to achieve this goal. Create a strategy for achieving this.

_____

_____

_____

_____

_____

_____

_____

Circle the 3 most important actions to take that would move you closer to achieving your goal.

Finally, if necessary, write all the additional actions you will need to take to complete each of the items you circled in the above space. This will be your action plan.

For example, if my top goal was to travel to Australia, one of the actions I would need to take is to make a detailed plan for the trip. To do this, I could speak with a travel agent, talk to others who have been to Australia, and research top tourist attractions there.

_____

_____

_____

_____

_____

_____

_____

Now put these actions on your calendar **RIGHT NOW**. Don't delay. You've already made a commitment; take action on it immediately!

Contribution and Legacy

In the space below, brainstorm all the things you would like to **contribute** in your life. This could include how or what you want to contribute, things you want to create, or how you want to be remembered.

This exercise can be challenging. If that's the case, consider asking yourself these questions to get you started: What have I done in the past in this area of my life that has been truly satisfying? What would happen if I did more of that?

_____

_____

_____

_____

_____

_____

_____

_____

_____

_____

_____

Next, circle the one, that if it came true, would have the biggest impact on your life in the next 12 months.

In the space below, write how achieving this goal will impact your life. What would it mean to you to reach this goal? What difference would it make? What emotions would you experience if you reached this goal?

_____

_____

_____

Next brainstorm all the actions that you need to take to achieve this goal. Create a strategy for achieving this.

_____

_____

_____

_____

_____

_____

_____

_____

Circle the 3 most important actions that would move you closer to achieving your goal.

Finally, if necessary, write all the subsequent actions you will need to take to complete each of the items you circled in the above space. This will be your action plan.

For example, if my top goal was to write a book on investing in stocks this year, one of my top actions might be to spend five hours per week writing the rough draft. Some additional actions may be outlining a plan of what to write, brainstorming the main ideas of the book, and researching current trends in blue chip stocks.

_____

_____

_____

_____

_____

_____

_____

_____

_____

Now put these actions on your calendar **RIGHT NOW.** Don't delay. You've already made a commitment; take action on it immediately!

Now, write your 5 goals from each section for the next year and underneath each goal write your top 3 actions to do.

_____

_____

_____

_____

_____

_____

_____

_____

_____

_____

_____

_____

_____

Figure out a way to review these goals DAILY. We tend to get what we focus on.

How will achieving ALL these goals this year make you feel? How will they impact your life? How committed are you to achieving them?

_____

_____

_____

_____

_____

Imagine you are 90 years old, sitting on your rocking chair and thinking about your life. You achieved all these goals. How does that make you feel? What if you never took action on any of these goals? Would you regret anything?

What resources do you have to achieve these goals? What resources will you need to achieve these goals?

Who can you find as a model for each of these goals? Is there someone you know or heard about who achieved a similar version of these goals?

Can you see any potential obstacles or barriers to achieving all of these goals? If so, how can you overcome them?

Are your current standards high enough to achieve all of these goals? If not, where do you need to set higher standards for yourself?

_____

_____

_____

_____

_____

Who must you become to achieve these goals and realize your life vision? What will your attitude be like? What do you value? How do you act? Who are you around? What is your mindset like?

_____

_____

_____

_____

_____

_____

_____

_____

_____

_____

_____

How will you celebrate once you achieve all of these goals?

_____

_____

_____

_____

How does each goal align with your top values?

_____

_____

_____

_____

_____

_____

_____

How can you achieve these goals while balancing your life as well?

_____

_____

_____

_____

_____

_____

_____

Envisioning Your Ideal Life

What would your life be like if it were exactly the way you wanted it to be? What would you change? What would you enhance? Who would you spend more or less time with? What would you do more or less of? How would you act? How would you spend your time? What are you like? What is your attitude like?

Think of the people, objects, work, feelings, and home that would make up your ideal life as a template.

It may be helpful to think in terms of the Wheel of Life categories. What would your ideal life look like in each of those categories on a weekly or consistent basis?

Write your answers to the above questions about your ideal life below.

_____

_____

_____

_____

_____

_____

_____

_____

_____

_____

_____

_____

_____

What are the 3-5 most important elements of your ideal life?

_____

_____

_____

Why do you want this lifestyle?

_____

_____

_____

_____

_____

_____

What do you need to do to achieve this ideal life? What action steps are required to achieve this? What abilities are required? Whose help do you need?

_____

_____

_____

_____

_____

_____

_____

Who do you need to become? What habits should you adopt? What do you need to learn? What should you practice?

_____

_____

_____

_____

_____

What are at least 5 things that you'd be doing on a regular basis?

_____

_____

_____

_____

What would your ideal weekly schedule look like? How many hours would you work? Which days would you work? How could you arrange your tasks to fit with your schedule best?

_____

_____

_____

_____

_____

What would others notice that's different about you in your ideal life than how you are now?

Are there any downsides to realizing this ideal future? If so, what are they?

What are the first steps you need to take in the next 1-6 months to get closer to this ideal life?

90 Day Goals in Various Areas of Life

Setting 90 day goals can be effective because it's much easier to take action and stay on track in a short, defined time frame. When you feel like you have a full year to achieve a goal, it becomes easy to procrastinate or put off working on it because it feels like there's a lot of time to reach that goal. When you set a 90 day goal, however, each day and each week are vital to reaching your objective, and the payoff comes much more quickly.

What areas of your life (up to 3) do you want to make progress in most in the next 90 days?

_____

_____

_____

For the first area, what specific result do you want in the next 90 days? Try to be as specific as possible.

_____

_____

_____

How will you know you have succeeded with this goal?

_____

_____

_____

Why MUST you make this happen? What are you willing to do to make this goal happen?

_____

_____

_____

What will it cost you NOT to reach this goal?

_____

_____

_____

What will you have to sacrifice to make room for this goal?

Next, create a MAP (Massive Action Plan) to achieve this 90 day goal.

List the **Actions** you MUST take to achieve this result. Then Prioritize the order in which they need to get done in the (P) column.

Assign a **Deadline** or date on your calendar when you will do each task.

Estimate how much **Time** each task will take to complete.

Then, schedule each action on your calendar.

P	Action/Task	Deadline	Time

What action(s) do you need to take THIS WEEK to be on track for your 90 day goal?

For the second area, what specific result do you want in the next 90 days? Try to be as specific as possible.

_____

_____

_____

_____

How will you know you have succeeded with this goal?

_____

_____

_____

Why MUST you make this happen? What are you willing to do to make this goal happen?

_____

_____

_____

What will it cost you NOT to reach this goal?

_____

_____

_____

What will you have to sacrifice to make room for this goal?

_____

_____

_____

Next, create a MAP (Massive Action Plan) to achieve this 90 day goal.

List the **Actions** you MUST take to achieve this result. Then Prioritize the order in which they need to get done in the (P) column.

Assign a **Deadline** or date on your calendar when you will do each task.

Estimate how much **Time** each task will take to complete.

Then, schedule each action on your calendar.

P	Action/Task	Deadline	Time

What action(s) do you need to take THIS WEEK to be on track for your 90 day goal?

_____

_____

_____

For the third area, what specific result do you want in the next 90 days? Try to be as specific as possible.

_____

_____

_____

How will you know you have succeeded with this goal?

_____

_____

_____

_____

Why MUST you make this happen? What are you willing to do to make this goal happen?

_____

_____

_____

_____

What will it cost you NOT to reach this goal?

_____

_____

_____

_____

What will you have to sacrifice to make room for this goal?

_____

_____

_____

_____

Next, create a MAP (Massive Action Plan) to achieve this 90 day goal.

List the **Actions** you MUST take to achieve this result. Then Prioritize the order in which they need to get done in the (P) column.

Assign a **Deadline** or date on your calendar when you will do each task.

Estimate how much **Time** each task will take to complete.

Then, schedule each action on your calendar.

P	Action/Task	Deadline	Time

What action(s) do you need to take THIS WEEK to be on track for your 90 day goal?

Accomplish a 5 Year Goal in 6 Months

What would it take for you to accomplish a 5 year goal in 6 months? This is a powerful question—and it leads to a powerful exercise. The question itself comes from Peter Thiel, the co-founder of PayPal.

Framing your thinking in this way will shift your focus to figuring out how to achieve your goals faster. The purpose of the exercise isn't necessarily to achieve the goal in 6 months, but to get you thinking about how you can be taking action on a bigger scale across the board.

Questions are powerful! When we ask a question, our minds automatically try to answer it. Often, simply asking a different or bigger question like this one can completely transform how you think.

What is your biggest 3-5 year goal?

_____

_____

_____

How can you accomplish your 3-5 year goal in the next 6 months? What would you need to do? Who would need to help you? What resources would you need? What mindset would you need to adopt?

_____

_____

_____

_____

_____

_____

_____

_____

_____

_____

How would you go about achieving this goal in a 6 month timeframe if you had unlimited resources?

How would achieving this goal change the quality of your life and the lives of others around you?

What's the first thing you would need to do to make this goal a reality?

What's the worse-case scenario from trying to achieve this goal in approximately 6 months? What's the upside?

If you are committed to achieving this goal, outline your action plan below.

Setting Some SMART Goals

The SMART format (**Specific, Measurable, Attainable, Relevant, Time-Specific**) is a tried and true method for setting goals. Let's make a few here.

Create 3 goals (or use goals from an earlier exercise). What exactly do you want to accomplish for each goal? Be **specific.**

_____

_____

_____

What will it look like when you reach your objective for each goal?

_____

_____

_____

How could you state these goals so your progress toward them is **measurable**? How can you quantify these goals so you'll know when you've reached them?

_____

_____

_____

_____

_____

_____

_____

_____

_____

Are there any barriers or circumstances that may hinder you from reaching these goals? If so, how can you plan to overcome them? How can you make **attaining** these goals possible?

_____

_____

_____

_____

_____

How important is achieving these goals? Why are they **relevant**? What are you willing to do to reach these goals?

_____

_____

_____

What's your deadline for achieving these goals? What **time-specific** framework are you working in? When will you start?

_____

_____

_____

What does your life look like once you've achieved these goals? What will a day in your life look like after you achieve these goals?

_____

_____

_____

_____

What emotions or feelings will you receive by achieving these goals?

_____

_____

_____

_____

How will reaching your goals impact others or the world in a positive way?

_____

_____

_____

_____

What will it cost NOT to reach your goals?

_____

_____

_____

_____

How will you celebrate once you achieve these goals?

_____

_____

_____

_____

Creating a MAP (Massive Action Plan)[5] (Goal 1)

In this exercise we will drill deeper into creating a plan to achieve a goal. Planning to achieve a goal can be a lot like baking a cake—if you follow a plan, strategy, or recipe, you'll get a specific outcome. To get that outcome, though, you have to follow the steps.

What is a goal that you really want to achieve? What is the specific result you're committed to achieving?

_____

_____

_____

Why do you really want it? Why are you committed to getting this result?

_____

_____

_____

_____

Brainstorm a list of specific actions that you must take to achieve this goal.

_____

_____

_____

_____

_____

5   Robbins, A. (2017). _Ultimate edge a three part system for creating an extraordinary life in any environment._ San Diego, CA: Robbins Research International.

Next, create a MAP (Massive Action Plan) to achieve this 90 day goal.

List the **Actions** you MUST take to achieve this result. Then Prioritize the order in which they need to get done in the (P) column.

Assign a **Deadline** or date on your calendar when you will do each task.

Estimate how much **Time** each task will take to complete.Then, <u>schedule each action on your calendar.</u>

P	Action/Task	Deadline	Time

All you have to do now is EXECUTE these actions.

Are there any obstacles to taking these actions and realizing your goal? If so, what are they? How will you overcome them?

_____

_____

_____

_____

How will you feel once you achieve this goal? How will it improve your life? How can you make taking these actions a MUST for you?

_____

_____

_____

Creating a MAP (Massive Action Plan) (Goal 2)

Pick another goal, ideally one that you have already created in a previous exercise.

What is a goal that you really want to achieve? What is the specific result you're committed to achieving?

Why do you really want it? Why are you committed to getting this result?

Brainstorm a list of specific actions that you must take to achieve this goal.

Next, create a MAP (Massive Action Plan) to achieve this 90 day goal.

List the **Actions** you MUST take to achieve this result. Then Prioritize the order in which they need to get done in the (P) column.

Assign a **Deadline** or date on your calendar when you will do each task.

Estimate how much **Time** each task will take to complete. Then, <u>schedule each action on your calendar.</u>

P	Action/Task	Deadline	Time

All you have to do now is EXECUTE these actions.

Are there any obstacles to taking these actions and realizing your goal? If so, what are they? How will you overcome them?

_____

_____

_____

_____

How will you feel once you achieve this goal? How will it improve your life? How can you make taking these actions a MUST for you?

_____

_____

_____

Creating a MAP (Massive Action Plan) (Goal 3)

Pick a third goal that you know you want to reach.

What is a goal that you really want to achieve? What is the specific result you're committed to achieving?

_____

_____

_____

Why do you really want it? Why are you committed to getting this result?

_____

_____

_____

Brainstorm a list of specific actions that you must take to achieve this goal.

_____

_____

_____

_____

_____

_____

_____

_____

_____

Next, create a MAP (Massive Action Plan) to achieve this 90 day goal.

List the **Actions** you MUST take to achieve this result. Then Prioritize the order in which they need to get done in the (P) column.

Assign a **Deadline** or date on your calendar when you will do each task.

Estimate how much **Time** each task will take to complete.

Then, schedule each action on your calendar.

P	Action/Task	Deadline	Time

All you have to do now is EXECUTE these actions.

Are there any obstacles to taking these actions and realizing your goal? If so, what are they? How will you overcome them?

_____

_____

_____

_____

How will you feel once you achieve this goal? How will it improve your life? How can you make taking these actions a MUST for you?

_____

_____

_____

Make More Money[6]

Brainstorm all the great things money can do for you, for those you love, and for others.

How can you earn 2-10 times more income while working the same amount of time? Some examples might be charging more per hour, asking for a raise, starting a business, investing, etc.

6   Robbins, A. (2013). *Awaken the giant within: How to take immediate control of your mental, emotional, physical & financial destiny!* New York: Simon & Schuster Paperbacks.

We are often paid in proportion to the amount of value we create for others. The concept of earning more money is simple: We just need to give or create more value.

How can you be worth more to your company, or how can you add more value to your customers? What skills or knowledge could you develop? What could you create?

Could you achieve more in less time? What about creating a better quality product or service? How can you improve current systems? How can you reach more people?

_____

_____

_____

_____

_____

_____

Which of these ideas are you committed to taking action on? What effect will they have on how much money you make? Outline your plan below.

_____

_____

_____

_____

_____

_____

Section Takeaways

What insights, breakthroughs, takeaways, and actionable items did you get from the above section?

NOTES

Section

Beliefs

W hat we believe about the world around us, about other people, about ourselves, and about our overall paradigm of reality has a tremendous impact on what actions we take, the emotional quality of our lives, and often determines how successful we will be in a given area.

Most people think that beliefs can't be changed, that they are stuck in their current way of thinking, feeling, or acting. This is not true. We all have the power to change ANY of the beliefs we have. All we must do is find enough evidence or experiences to support the new belief.

In this section, you will dive deeper into what your most limiting and empowering beliefs are. You will then work to eradicate your most limiting beliefs and work to condition your empowering beliefs. You will also create a new identity for yourself and develop metaphors for how you view life as a whole.

Changing Your Limiting Beliefs and Discovering Empowering Ones

"A limiting belief is a state of mind, conviction, or perception that you think to be true that limits you in some way. This limiting belief could be about you, your interactions with other people, or with the world and how it works."[7]

Limiting beliefs prevent us from pursuing our goals and desires and hinder us from reaching our potential. These beliefs might sound like: I will fail if I try _____, I will never be successful at _____, or I'm not good enough for _____.

Brainstorm all the limiting beliefs that you have (or at least your most limiting beliefs).

_____

_____

_____

_____

_____

_____

_____

_____

_____

_____

_____

_____

_____

Circle your top 3-5 limiting beliefs.

---

7   Dan Matthews, C. (2020, December 10). How to identify your limiting beliefs and get over them. Retrieved April 14, 2021, from https://www.lifehack.org/858652/limiting-beliefs#:~:text=A%20limiting%20belief%20is%20a,of%20 negative%20effects%20on%20you.

What negative experiences have you encountered as a result of these beliefs? How have these beliefs limited you?

_____

_____

_____

_____

_____

Next, ask, "How is this belief ridiculous or absurd?" for each of the limiting beliefs you circled.

_____

_____

_____

_____

_____

_____

Finally, ask, "What will it cost me (physically, emotionally, relationally, financially, etc.) if I don't let go of this belief?"

_____

_____

_____

_____

_____

_____

_____

Now, write down a replacement for each of these beliefs (often it's the exact opposite of what the limiting belief is). These will now be empowering beliefs for you. For example, suppose one limiting belief was, "Raising money is hard for me." The empowering alternative is "Raising money is easy for me!"

_____

_____

_____

_____

What references do you have to back up these new, empowering beliefs? What references do you need to gain that support your new, empowering beliefs?

_____

_____

_____

_____

_____

_____

_____

_____

The next step is to say these new, empowering beliefs at least once per day for the next 30 days. Say them with emotion and confidence! Repeating them will program the new beliefs into your nervous system. If we repeat something long enough, eventually we begin to believe it.

The opposite of a limiting belief is an empowering belief. These are beliefs, convictions, states of mind, or perceptions about yourself, others, and the world in general that give you confidence, put you in a better emotional state, or empower you in some way.

Brainstorm all the empowering beliefs you currently have.

_____

_____

_____

_____

_____

_____

_____

_____

Circle 3-5 of your most empowering beliefs from the list above.

What positive experiences have you encountered from these beliefs? How have they empowered you?

_____

_____

_____

_____

_____

_____

_____

_____

_____

_____

What references or experiences do you have that support these beliefs?

_____

_____

_____

_____

_____

_____

_____

_____

How will these beliefs help you in life?

_____

_____

_____

_____

_____

_____

_____

_____

Reviewing Important References and Gaining New Ones

References are books, people, quotations, stories, insights, or life experiences that serve as emotional or intellectual touchstones for you. What are the top 5-10 experiences or references that have shaped your life? How did they impact you?

What are some experiences or references that could help you succeed at the highest level, and achieve what you really want in life?

_____

_____

_____

_____

_____

_____

_____

_____

Assign a deadline for each of the experiences or references you named. Map out strategies and action steps for gaining these new experiences or references below.

_____

_____

_____

_____

_____

_____

_____

_____

_____

_____

_____

_____

Creating Your New Identity

Our identities are powerful: who we believe we are at our core shapes everything we do. Often, our emotions and actions are influenced by this identity as well.

We find our identity through our occupation, our social roles, personality, values, spirituality, and more. Think of a soldier as an example—the identity of a solider is often one that is tough, disciplined, masculine, self-sacrificing, and works to serve the common good.

In the space below, write how you would define yourself. What is your identity? What is the essence of who you are? What roles do you play?

_____

_____

_____

_____

_____

_____

_____

Who do you want to be? Make a list of all the elements of your desired identity.

_____

_____

_____

_____

_____

_____

Now, develop an action plan to achieve this new identity. How would you act? What would you do? Who would you hang out with? What habits would be a part of your life? What would your attitude be like?

_____

_____

_____

_____

_____

_____

_____

_____

_____

How committed are you to achieving this new identity? What are you willing to do to be this person?

_____

_____

_____

Look at your new identity description daily until it becomes wired into you.

Creating Affirmations[8]

Affirmations are empowering beliefs or statements, things you want to manifest in your life, goals to achieve, emotions to gain or lose, Bible verses, and so much more.

In general, there are 5 types of affirmations:

Releasing /Cleansing: help you let go of unwanted emotions and purify your system.

I let go of _____

Receiving/Accepting: allow something to be.

I accept, I am open to, I allow _____

Being/Intending: ground your purpose, enhance your intention, and deepen your understanding.

My intention is, my goal is, I live _____

Acting/Claiming: bring something into manifestation and help you claim power.

I act, I demand, I am, I make _____

Integrating/Embodying: allow energy to merge with your physiology.

Today is, I breathe, I radiate, I display, I embody _____

In the space below, come up with as many affirmations as you can that relate to the five categories above.

_____

_____

_____

_____

_____

_____

_____

_____

8 Williams, P., & Menendez, D. S. (2015). Becoming a professional life coach: Lessons from the institute for life coach training. New York, NY: W.W. Norton & Company.

Out of this list, **circle the top 10 affirmations that have the most emotional impact for you**.

Read, write, or speak them daily. I would HIGHLY recommend speaking them with passion and emotion. Combining emotion and passion with your affirmations helps them get wired into your nervous system quicker. Repeat these until they become fused with your physiology, and a habitual way of thinking, acting, or believing.

Identifying Your Life Metaphors

The metaphors that we attribute to life as a whole are yet another set of powerful beliefs that we have. Someone who views life as a gift will approach life very differently from someone who views it as one big party.

Think deeply about what metaphors you have about life, whether they are your own, what you were raised to believe growing up, or by the culture around you.

What metaphors describe your attitude toward life? What metaphors do you have for life itself?

_____

_____

_____

_____

Where do you think these metaphors come from? What do they imply about your attitude toward life?

_____

_____

_____

_____

Are there any new metaphors you'd like to adopt about life? What would they be? What are some you could use that are more suited to your values?

_____

_____

_____

_____

Section Takeaways

What insights, breakthroughs, takeaways, and actionable items did you get from the above section?

7

Emotions

O ne of my mentors, Tony Robbins, often says that, "The quality of your emotions dictates the quality of your life." There is a lot of truth to that statement. It doesn't matter how much money you have, how many people like you, or how successful you are, if you are constantly experiencing negative emotional states then you're not going to have a high quality of life.

In this section, you will identify which emotional states you operate in most frequently. You will work to limit the amount of time you spend in negative emotional states and increase the amount of time you experience positive emotional states. Then, you will look at how you can eliminate some stress in your life.

Changing Unwanted Emotions[9]

Brainstorm a list of all the emotions you experience in an average week. (Most people range between 8-14 emotions on an average week). Try not to list more than 20 or so.

_____

_____

_____

_____

_____

_____

_____

Mark whether each emotion is positive, negative, or neutral.

_____

_____

_____

Next, list the events, situations, or people that trigger these emotions most of the time.

_____

_____

_____

_____

9 Robbins, A. (2013). Awaken the giant within: How to take immediate control of your mental, emotional, physical & financial destiny! New York: Simon & Schuster Paperbacks.

How do each of these emotions affect your behavior?

_____

_____

_____

_____

_____

_____

_____

_____

Now, come up with a remedy for each negative emotion. How could you quickly shift or reframe this emotion? Is there a way to get into a positive state instead? Is there a different word or meaning you could use to describe it? Could you change your belief about this emotion? How can you break out of these negative emotional patterns for the long term?

For example, suppose a common emotion for me is stress from work. I could replace "Stressed" with "Energized" by thinking of all the opportunities I get to work on exciting projects and to learn new things.

Some other ideas may be to play music that puts me in a good mood, meditate, pray, or create a list of all the things I'm grateful for.

How can you reframe your negative emotions?

_____

_____

_____

_____

_____

How will you respond when negative emotion arises in the future?

_____

_____

_____

_____

_____

_____

_____

Here are some additional questions to help you change your negative emotional patterns and states.

What are these emotions trying to tell you? What messages are they trying to send you?

For example, fear is often a signal that we need to prepare for something that may come up in the future.

_____

_____

_____

_____

_____

_____

_____

_____

How do you really want to feel instead? What would you need to believe to feel that way now? What are you willing to do to change these emotions?

_____

_____

_____

_____

_____

_____

_____

What's great about feeling each of these emotions and what can you learn from them?

_____

_____

_____

_____

_____

_____

_____

_____

_____

How to Feel Good Instantly

Brainstorm a list of things you can do that have an immediate positive impact on how you feel.

Examples might include playing music you really enjoy, going outside for a walk, making a list of all the things you are grateful for, calling a friend, getting a massage, doing a hobby you enjoy, watching a movie, etc.

_____

_____

_____

_____

_____

_____

_____

_____

_____

_____

_____

How can you incorporate these activities into your life more regularly? In what situations would it be appropriate to do some of these activities?

_____

_____

_____

_____

_____

Energy Drains and Gains

List some of the things both at work and at home that drain you. They could be little annoyances, relationships, people, or big problems.

It may be helpful to think in terms of the wheel of life areas:

Health/Body
Career/Business
Finances
Relationships/Family

Time Management
Emotions
Social/Fun/Self-Care
Personal/Spiritual Development

Next, create a plan for working to eradicate one or more of these items each week. Prioritize them in the order you want eliminated from your life.

_____

_____

_____

_____

_____

_____

_____

_____

Create a list of things that give you energy—both at home and at work. These could be people, activities, hobbies, etc.

_____

_____

_____

_____

_____

_____

_____

_____

Which of these can you do more of each week? What specifically would that look like? Which energy gains do you want to prioritize?

Eliminating Some Stress in Your life

Make a list of 10 promises, obligations, or other things that cause unwanted stress in your life.

Where have you set yourself up for unwanted stress and failure? What perceptions or situations do you experience that consistently cause you stress in a negative way?

_____

_____

_____

_____

_____

_____

_____

What alternatives could you pursue? How can you step away from some of the unwanted obligations you signed up for?

_____

_____

_____

_____

_____

_____

What are the top 3 sources of stress in your life? What specifically makes them stressful for you?

_____

_____

_____

_____

What about these situations are not in your control?

_____

_____

_____

_____

What about these situations are in your control?

_____

_____

_____

_____

How can you eliminate or greatly reduce each of these sources of stress in your life?

_____

_____

_____

_____

How would it feel if these sources of stress were eliminated once and for all?

_____

_____

_____

_____

What are some negative coping mechanisms you have used in the past to cope with stress or lower your stress levels? For example, drinking alcohol or mistreating others when you're stressed would be a negative coping mechanism.

_____

_____

_____

_____

What are some positive things you can adopt or you have done to cope with stress? For example, working out or meditating when stressed would be a positive coping mechanism.

_____

_____

_____

_____

Can you identify at least 5 positive methods for coping with stress that you would like to make a permanent part of your daily or weekly life? List them below.

_____

_____

_____

_____

_____

Section Takeaways

What insights, breakthroughs, takeaways, and actionable items did you get from the above section?

NOTES

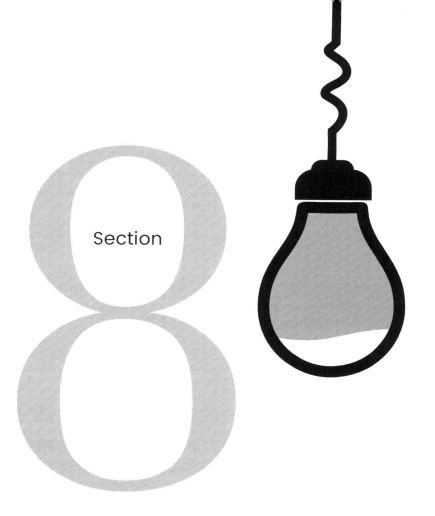

Section

Habits + Routines

L ike boundaries, habits and routines are pre-determined decisions that don't take much thought or energy to maintain once you've built up enough momentum and consistency. When we lack consistency, life is inevitably more chaotic, which can make it much harder to grow.

Being successful often boils down to creating the right habits and routines. In this section, you will identify certain habits and routines you want to create and which ones you want to eliminate. You will also use pain, pleasure, and neuro-associations to help condition these habits so they become integrated into your life more easily.

Creating a Morning Routine

To have a calmer, more focused, and more productive day, it's important to take some time to practice positive morning rituals. A morning routine will help you get into a more effective state of mind than just rolling out of bed.

Think of your morning routine as a way to stretch or warm up before exercising: if you jump straight into exercising without warming up, you're at greater risk of injury. On the other hand, taking a few minutes to stretch loosens your muscles, increases the effectiveness of your workout, and helps prevent injury.

A morning ritual is your way to stretch and warm up yourself before taking on the day, making it more likely that you'll approach the day effectively.

Start by describing your current morning schedule. What time do you get up? What activities take place on a regular basis? About how long does each activity take?

_____

_____

_____

_____

_____

Now think about the activities you would like to incorporate into your morning routine. Some examples might be exercising, reading, praying or meditating, saying affirmations, journaling, doing a hobby, etc.

_____

_____

_____

_____

_____

Now, create a morning schedule that will allow you to incorporate this extra time for these activities. It may require that you wake up earlier. What activities from the list above will you include? In what order will you do them? How long will you do each activity on average?

_____

_____

_____

_____

_____

Try this new morning routine out for a few weeks to see how it improves the quality of your day. You can always tweak it by adding or reducing the activities, the duration of each activity, or the time you have allotted for your schedule.

Changing and Creating Habits

What are three habits that you would either like to change or incorporate into your life? Choose 3 habits:

1. A habit that will benefit you personally

2. A habit related to business or work

3. A habit that will be of service to someone else

_____

_____

_____

_____

_____

How can you remind yourself to do (or not do) this each day? What structures would you put in place to make sure you do (or don't do) this consistently?

_____

_____

_____

_____

_____

What would it cost you if you don't change (if you don't incorporate this new habit or action into your life)? What pain would you experience by not changing?

_____

_____

_____

_____

What's something you could reward yourself with once you complete these habits? It could be a daily, weekly, or periodic reward.

_____

_____

_____

_____

_____

If you are trying to eliminate a habit, what's something you could replace it with instead? Something that would give you pleasure.

_____

_____

_____

_____

_____

Who can keep you accountable with these habits? What will you ask this person to do for you?

_____

_____

_____

_____

What can you do today to incorporate these habits into your life?

_____

_____

_____

_____

_____

Changing Negative Neuro-Associations[10]

Neuro-associations are deep-rooted associations that our brains form between two things. Some examples could be that eating chocolate equates to feeling happy, exercising equals pain, or getting nervous when you see your boss walking to your desk.

We have neuro-associations for many things in our lives, but most people have never examined what their major neuro-associations are.

What are 3 neuro-associations that you've made in the past that have positively impacted your life? These could be associations like linking exercise and pleasure, getting excited about saving money, or enjoying the process of learning new things.

_____

_____

_____

_____

What are 3 neuro-associations that you've made in the past that have negatively impacted your life? These could be associations like linking pain with taking risks, getting nervous when starting conversations with strangers, or enjoying eating unhealthy food.

_____

_____

_____

_____

What negative neuro-associations are affecting or limiting you most now?

_____

_____

_____

_____

_____

_____

10   Robbins, A. (2017). *Ultimate edge a three part system for creating an extraordinary life in any environment*. San Diego, CA: Robbins Research International.

How can you change these negative neuro-associations? What new habits or conditioning could you implement to interrupt these patterns?

Two common methods are rewarding yourself for doing the opposite of the neuro-association, or using something painful to interrupt the pattern. I heard of someone who used wet cat food as a motivator to stop eating sweets. If she slipped up on eating dessert, she vowed to eat a can of wet cat food! Something like that will certainly motivate you to think twice about grabbing dessert.

Section Takeaways

What insights, breakthroughs, takeaways, and actionable items did you get from the above section?

_____

_____

_____

_____

_____

_____

_____

_____

_____

_____

_____

_____

_____

_____

_____

_____

_____

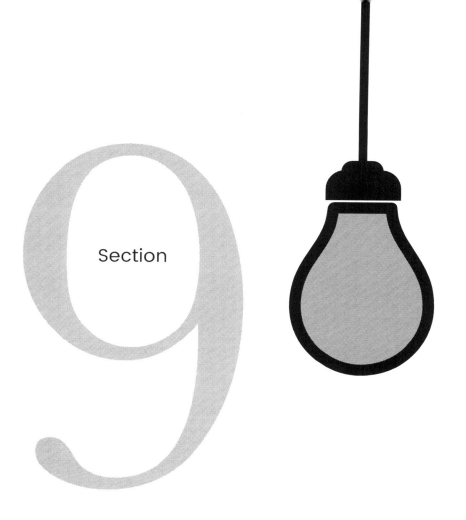

Section

Relationships

Relationships are an essential component of a happy, healthy, and well-rounded life. Whether it's a relationship with a partner, friends, family, or a spiritual relationship, life needs connections and things to share with others. Our relationships offer us the opportunity to share a piece of who we are and to learn from one another.

In this section, you will assess several of your current key relationships. Once you know exactly what you want to get and give in each of your relationships, you can put an action plan into place. Then, you will consider how you can add to and leverage your network, and assess your spiritual relationships.

Relationship Assessment

What are your top relationships? Who do you spend the most time with and how would you rate the quality of each of those relationships?

_____

_____

_____

_____

_____

_____

_____

What do you contribute to each relationship?

_____

_____

_____

_____

_____

_____

_____

What are the most positive characteristics that you bring to your relationships? What are your greatest qualities and skills within your relationships?

_____

_____

_____

_____

Are there any new skills or qualities you want to develop in your relationships? If so, how can you develop them?

Which relationship do you most want to improve? Why?

What would that improvement look like?

How can you contribute to improving this relationship? What action steps can you take?

_____

_____

_____

_____

_____

_____

_____

How committed are you to making these contributions even if the other person doesn't contribute any more than they currently are?

_____

_____

_____

What relationship(s) in your life is being neglected? How could you nurture it?

_____

_____

_____

_____

_____

_____

Think of 3 high quality relationships you have or have had in your life. What makes or made them great? Are there any themes or attributes you could apply to other relationships?

_____

_____

_____

_____

_____

What relationship, if any, would you like in your life right now that you don't currently have? What can you do to create it?

_____

_____

_____

_____

If you were in a relationship with yourself, how would it feel? What's it like to be in a relationship with you?

_____

_____

_____

_____

_____

_____

_____

_____

Closing the Gap In a Relationship

Think of a relationship that you want to improve or develop.

Where are you currently at in this relationship? How would you assess it? What is working well and what isn't going so well?

_____

_____

_____

_____

_____

_____

_____

Where do you want to be in this relationship? Visualize your ideal relationship. What would it look like? What would you talk about, share, or do together?

_____

_____

_____

_____

_____

_____

_____

_____

What actions can you take to get there? Which ones are most important for you to take?

How will improving this relationship affect other areas of your life?

How committed are you to creating this desired relationship? What are you willing to do for it? What are you willing to sacrifice for it?

Adding to Your Network

Who are the 10-15 people you communicate with most often? What category is each person in (family, friend, work colleague, partner, etc.)?

_____

_____

_____

_____

_____

_____

What are you doing or what could you be doing to add goodwill to each of these relationships?

_____

_____

_____

_____

_____

_____

What category do you want more or better relationships in? Why? Are there any gaps in your current network?

_____

_____

_____

How can you find new people to add into various areas of your network? Where would you go, what would you do, and how could you connect with others? Is there anyone that you've had a past relationship with that you could reignite?

Relationship with Your Creator

How would you assess your relationship with God? If you are not religious, how would you assess your spiritual relationship or your relationship to the world around you?

_____

_____

_____

_____

What would an ideal relationship with your Creator feel and look like for you? What would an ideal spiritual relationship feel and look like?

_____

_____

_____

_____

_____

_____

What actions can you take to create this desired relationship? Which ones will you commit to?

_____

_____

_____

_____

_____

How can you become more aligned with your spiritual nature? How can you exercise it more?

_____

_____

_____

_____

_____

What aspects of your spiritual life do you want to strengthen? How can you achieve this?

_____

_____

_____

_____

_____

Section Takeaways

What insights, breakthroughs, takeaways, and actionable items did you get from the above section?

_____

_____

_____

_____

_____

_____

_____

_____

_____

_____

_____

_____

_____

_____

_____

_____

Section

Ending Exercises

In this final section, you will sum up what all you've learned from the previous exercises and review your takeaways from each section. You will identify what breakthroughs, insights, and new actions you will start to implement into your life.

I suggest that you flip through your answers from the previous exercises to see what really stuck out to you, and what your most important actions to take will be going forward.

Gratitude List

It's impossible to be fearful and grateful at the same time. Create a list of things you are grateful for below. Refer to this list when times get tough or you're having a bad day.

_____

_____

_____

_____

_____

_____

_____

_____

_____

_____

_____

_____

_____

_____

_____

_____

_____

_____

Wrapping Up What You Learned

My top 3-5 goals for this next year are:

_____

_____

_____

_____

_____

Here are the action steps I will take to complete them:

_____

_____

_____

_____

_____

_____

_____

_____

_____

_____

_____

_____

I'm committed to achieving these goals because:

_____

_____

_____

_____

My purpose (as best I know) is:

_____

_____

_____

_____

My top going-towards values are:

_____

_____

_____

_____

My top empowering beliefs are:

_____

_____

_____

_____

_____

What I've learned from all these exercises is:

_____

_____

_____

_____

_____

_____

_____

_____

_____

_____

I'm most excited about:

_____

_____

_____

_____

_____

The biggest change(s) I will be making in my life is:

_____

_____

_____

_____

_____

The major breakthroughs I've gotten from this workbook are:

_____

_____

_____

_____

_____

_____

_____

_____

I can apply what I've learned from these exercises to other aspects of my life by:

_____

_____

_____

_____

_____

I will ensure these positive changes will stick because:

Final Thoughts

Congratulations! You've made it to the end of this workbook! By now, I hope you have had multiple breakthroughs that will help you change your life for the better. If you haven't already, start taking action on what you've learned. The quicker you start putting it into practice, the quicker you will start to see real changes in your life.

I also think it would be wise to review your answers to these exercises. Now that you have completed most or all of these exercises, you will have more clarity about how everything comes together to make positive changes in your life.

If I can ever be of assistance to you through my coaching services to help you build on the momentum from this workbook, or you would like to connect with me, the best way to reach me is through email. You can email me at: hunter@huntercarsoncoaching.com.

I wish you much success in your life, and if our paths ever cross, I hope to learn about the changes you've made!

To Transforming Your Life,

Hunter Carson

Huntercarsoncoaching.com

References

Dan Matthews, C. (2020, December 10). How to identify your limiting beliefs and get over them. Retrieved April 14, 2021, from https://www.lifehack.org/858652/limiting-beliefs#:~:text=A%20 limiting%20belief%20is%20a,of%20negative%20effects%20on%20you.

Martin, C. (2001). The life coaching handbook: Everything you need to be an effective life coach. Carmarthen, Wales, UK: Crown House Publishing limited.

Robbins, A. (2013). Awaken the giant within: How to take immediate control of your mental, emotional, physical & financial destiny! New York: Simon & Schuster Paperbacks.

Robbins, A. (2017). Ultimate edge a three part system for creating an extraordinary life in any environment. San Diego, CA: Robbins Research International.

Robbins, T. (2020). The gap map. Retrieved April 14, 2021, from https://gapmap.tonyrobbins.com/

Stoltzfus, T. (2008). Coaching questions: A coach's guide to powerful asking skills. Virginia Beach, VA: Tony Stoltzfus.

Williams, P., & Menendez, D. S. (2015). Becoming a professional life coach: Lessons from the institute for life coach training. New York, NY: W.W. Norton & Company.

Williams, P., & Thomas, L. J. (2005). Total life coaching: 50+ life lessons, skills and techniques to enhance your practice-- and your life. New York, NY: W.W. Norton.

Made in the USA
Columbia, SC
31 October 2024

45065461R00098